189/285

THE WORLD OF
THE BRONTËS

THE WORLD OF
THE BRONTËS

Photographed by Paul Barker
Commentary by James Birdsall

PAVILION

ACKNOWLEDGEMENTS

In addition to all those people who have written about the Brontës in the past century and a half, we would especially like to thank Wendy, Tracey, George and Sue in the Library for their cheerful help and tolerance.

PAUL BARKER AND JAS BIRDSALL

First published in Great Britain in 1996 by

PAVILION BOOKS LIMITED

26 Upper Ground, London SE1 9PD

Text copyright © James Birdsall 1996

Photographs copyright © Paul Barker 1996

Designed by Nigel Partridge

The moral right of the author has been asserted.

A CIP catalogue record for this book is available from the British Library.

ISBN 1 85793 687 6

Typeset in Centaur

Printed and bound in Spain by Bookprint

2 4 6 8 10 9 7 5 3 1

This book may be ordered by post direct from the publisher. Please contact the Marketing Department. But try your bookshop first.

FRONTISPIECE: *Wycoller.*

Contents

About this Book

The places featured in this book, with their relevance to the Brontës, are not set in any historical sequence. Apart from Hartshead and Thornton, which very properly start it, they radiate out from Haworth as a central focus, progressing further away as you turn the pages. There are no detailed directions, for these get in the way. You can be so busy looking for the path that you miss the panorama. Most of the places are easy enough to find anyway.

Many of the associations with the literature are based on guesswork. After all, the 'Bells' kept their own identity – even their gender – a secret for long enough, let alone divulging their sources of inspiration. So there are three Thornfield Halls? And just where was Wuthering Heights? This book does not tell you, but it might give you the pleasure of deciding for yourself.

INTRODUCTION

My first reaction to the suggestion for yet another book about the Brontës was a feeling that I was quite the wrong person to undertake it. I had been a philistine all my life, where the works of Currer, Ellis and Acton Bell were concerned; in the current vernacular, I had been since childhood a positive Brontë-sceptic. I had heard about the family from my Yorkshire grandparents, who had known people who remembered the Brontës, but I found infinitely depressing the images conjured up by the black, precipitous little village where consumption reigned and by the bleak, featureless gritstone moor above it. The sun never shone on either when I visited them, and I must have believed – erroneously – that it never did. So somehow the novels eluded me in my early years and, happily, no essential reading list or didactic syllabus of my schooldays forced them to my attention. Only one splendid hymn, 'No Coward Soul is Mine', stirred my young being to the core, and it was with surprise that I discovered it to be a poem by Emily Brontë.

Shared experience is the beginning of empathy. As a schoolboy at Sedbergh in 1952, skating with two friends on a limpid, crackling February morning, I saw three suns in the cloudless sky. They were in line horizontally, well apart and equally spaced, and all seemed of comparable brightness. The phenomenon lasted some twenty minutes, after which the outer pair of suns faded and disappeared. Portents of Judgement Day vied with recent memory of the Hiroshima bomb, but our alarm was short-lived. Over the years the incident faded from my mind, just as the supplementary suns had done from the blue sky. But in the course of my research for this book I discovered that in August 1847 the three Brontë sisters and their friend, Ellen Nussey, witnessed the same spectacle from Haworth Moor. This was shortly after *Wuthering Heights* and *Agnes Grey* had been accepted for publication and just prior to the acceptance of *Jane Eyre.* Ellen likened the sisters to the three suns in the sky. Charlotte was worried by the comparison, but Emily wore a happy, secret smile.

I discovered that the phenomenon is termed the Parhelion and, though a rare occurrence, has been witnessed from Haworth periodically over the past 500 years. The scene they described impressed me vividly. I might have been there. Since then, I have come to know the sisters well – the shy Anne, the prim, determined Charlotte and the deep, mysterious Emily.

I said that 'happily' the novels were never thrust upon me at an early age. Instead, I have come to them later, when my faculties of understanding, insight and (dare I say it?) criticism have become more fully developed than those of the neophyte juggling with the various disciplines demanded by School Certificate in my day, or the equivalent of today's GCSEs and A-levels. Separated from their background, the works are succulent fare enough. Re-read with a knowledge of the isolation, the paucity of experience, the confined social intercourse of the Brontë sisters, their intuitive genius becomes staggering. And yet there is an underlying simplicity that can reach the heart of any reader, old or young, worldly-wise or unsophisticated. This is probably the essence of genius. When I read of the landscape around Lowood School, the disturbing description of Filey Brigg in *Shirley*, Cathy's wistful picture of a favourite summer day in *Wuthering Heights* — all sites familiar to me — behind my enjoyment hide, first the satisfaction that, separated by a century, we all saw the three suns, and then the ghost of Emily's secret smile.

To people who believe, as I do, that places retain an aura of those who have immortalized them, this book is dedicated. The world has moved on immeasurably since Haworth Parsonage housed the unpre-tentious family that was destined to spread its fame throughout it. It is strange to realize today that *Jane Eyre* was once generally considered a 'naughty book'; that local people opined indignantly that *Wuthering Heights* was a scurrilous smear on the district. But the Yorkshire landscapes, especially the skylines, abide unaltered, and many of the remaining houses preserve the appearance that they presented to Charlotte, and which inspired Briarmains, Thornfield and the rest. Haworth itself seems at first glance radically changed with the times. But raise your eyes above the shop signs and the Brontë hysteria: the old rooftops still form the patterns that the Brontës themselves would recognize.

JAMES BIRDSALL, YORKSHIRE 1995

✶

RIGHT: Yeoman Hill.

MAIN EVENTS IN THE LIVES OF THE BRONTË FAMILY

1777 The Reverend Patrick Brontë was born in County Down, Eire.

1783 Maria Branwell was born in Penzance.

1812 In the spring Patrick Brontë was appointed examiner at nearby Woodhouse Grove School. In June he met Maria, niece of the headmaster, who came from Cornwall to stay at the school. In August he proposed to her on a visit to Kirkstall Abbey and was accepted. They were married before the end of the year.

1814 In early January their eldest daughter, Maria, was born at Hightown, near Liversedge.

1815 On 8 February their second daughter, Elizabeth, was born at Hightown. On 19 May Patrick Brontë exchanged the living at Hartshead for that of Thornton.

1816 Charlotte was born at Thornton vicarage on 21 April.

1817 Their son, Patrick Branwell, was born at Thornton on 26 June.

1818 Emily was born at Thornton on 30 July.

1820 Anne was born at Thornton on 17 January. On 20 April the family moved to the Parsonage at Haworth.

1821 Mrs Maria Brontë had by now become terminally ill with cancer. In May her sister, Elizabeth (Aunt Branwell), came to look after her and the family. On 15 September Maria died.

1824 The two elder daughters, Maria and Elizabeth, went to the Reverend Carus Wilson's school at Cowan Bridge on 1 July. On 10 August Charlotte joined them. On 2 September the three younger children witnessed a huge landslip on the moors above Haworth. Emily joined her sisters at Cowan Bridge School on 25 November.

1825 Early in the year there was an outbreak of 'low fever' (typhoid) at Cowan Bridge. At the Parsonage, 'Tabby' (Tabitha Aykroyd) came to the Brontës as cook. On 14 February Maria, terminally ill, was sent home from school. She died on 6 May. Elizabeth was also very ill and sent home on 31 May, followed in a few days by Charlotte and Emily. Elizabeth died on 15 June.

1826 Charlotte wrote her first story, for Anne, who was probably also ill.

1829 In December Branwell painted his famous 'Gun Group' picture (see inset on front of jacket), originally showing himself and his three sisters. He later painted himself out.

1831 Charlotte went to Miss Margaret Wooler's school at Roe Head, Mirfield, on 17 January. Here she first met her lifelong friends, Ellen Nussey and Mary Taylor. In mid-May Branwell walked from Haworth to see them – there and back a distance of some forty miles. In June he started taking boxing lessons from John Brown at the Black Bull.

1832 In May Charlotte left Roe Head to teach Emily and Anne at home. In September she and Branwell visited Ellen Nussey at her home, Rydings, at Birstall. In the same year Reverend Brontë built the Sunday School near the Parsonage. Charlotte became the first superintendent.

1833 On 8 April Reverend Brontë joined the Keighley Mechanics' Institute. In September Ellen Nussey came to the Parsonage for her first visit. The family took her on a visit to Bolton Abbey and the Priory.

1835 On 29 July Charlotte returned to Roe Head as a teacher, taking Emily with her as a pupil. Emily was severely homesick and returned to the Parsonage in mid-October.

1836 In January Anne took Emily's place at Roe Head.

1837 In July Miss Wooler moved her school to Heald's House, Dewsbury Moor, to which Charlotte and Anne returned in August after the holidays. By December Anne was unwell and they both went home to the Parsonage.

1838 In May Branwell set himself up in a studio in Bradford as a portrait painter. On 23 May Charlotte finally left Miss Wooler's school. In September Emily went as a music teacher to Law Hill, Southowram. In December Charlotte visited Ellen Nussey at her new home, Brookroyd, in Batley.

1839 In March or early April Emily came home from Law Hill. On 8 April Anne went as governess to the Ingham family at Blake Hall, Mirfield. In May Charlotte went as governess to the Sidgwicks at Stonegappe, Lothersdale, and Branwell gave up his studio and returned home. In mid-September Charlotte and Ellen went on a seaside holiday to Easton House, Burlington, now Bridlington. It was Charlotte's first

view of the sea. Anne left Blake Hall in December, and on New Year's Eve Branwell went as tutor to the Postlethwaite family at Broughton-in-Furness near Ulverston.

1840 On 1 May Branwell visited Hartley Coleridge, poet, at Ambleside. On 31 August he was appointed assistant clerk-in-charge at Sowerby Bridge railway station. The station and its line opened on 5 October.

1841 In March Anne went as governess to the Robinsons at Thorp Green Hall, Little Ouseburn, near York. Charlotte went as governess to Mrs White of Upperwood House, Rawdon. On 1 April Branwell was transferred to Luddenden Foot railway station as clerk-in-charge. In mid-July Anne went on holiday to Scarborough with her employers. On Christmas Eve Charlotte left Rawdon.

1842 In February Charlotte and Emily went to be further educated at M. Héger's establishment in Brussels. On 29 October 'Aunt Branwell' died at the Parsonage. Charlotte and Emily returned to Haworth on 8 November.

1843 Anne returned to Thorp Green in January, taking Branwell with her as tutor. On 27 January Charlotte returned to Brussels by herself.

1844 On 3 January Charlotte returned home to Haworth.

1845 In mid-June Anne left Thorp Green. Charlotte went to Hathersage with Ellen to prepare the vicarage for her brother, Henry Nussey. On 17 July Branwell was dismissed from his employment at Thorp Green for 'proceedings bad beyond expression'. In early October Charlotte, Emily and Anne chose to publish a selection of their own poems at their own expense, under the *noms de plume* Currer, Ellis and Acton Bell. The autumn was spent writing their novels: *The Professor* (Charlotte); *Wuthering Heights* (Emily) and *Agnes Grey* (Anne).

1846 Early in the year the novels were still being written. As his alcoholism increased, Branwell's health was seriously deteriorating, compounded by an increasing addiction to opium. Late May saw the publication of the poems of Currer, Ellis and Acton Bell, which were reviewed in *The Athenaeum* on 4 July. In late August Charlotte accompanied her father to Manchester, where he underwent an eye operation for cataract. They stayed at 83 Mount Pleasant, Boundary Street, Oxford Road, where Charlotte started to write *Jane Eyre.* They returned to Haworth on 28 September.

1847 Early in July the publishers T. C. Newby accepted *Wuthering Heights* and *Agnes Grey*, but rejected *The Professor*. On 6 August, the publishers Smith, Elder & Co. rejected *The Professor,* but expressed interest in another novel by Charlotte. She sent them the manuscript of *Jane Eyre* and on 24 August they unhesitatingly accepted it. In September, on a visit to Ellen, Charlotte covertly corrected the proofs. On 16 October *Jane Eyre* was published under the pseudonym of Currer Bell, to immediate acclaim. Early in December *Wuthering Heights* and *Agnes Grey* were published under the respective pen-names of Ellis Bell and Acton Bell.

1848 In January *Jane Eyre* went into its second edition, and in April its third. In July Anne's second novel, *The Tenant of Wildfell Hall*, was published. On 8 July Charlotte and Anne went to London to visit Smith, Elder & Co. George Smith, their publisher, took them to Covent Garden to hear *The Barber of Seville* and they later visited the Royal Academy and the National Portrait Gallery. During the year Branwell became progressively iller, both physically and mentally, and on 24 September he died. By October both Emily and Charlotte were very ill. Emily became gravely weak with tuberculosis of the lungs, obstinately refusing the services of a doctor. On 19 December she at last consented to see one, but died at 2 p.m.

1849 On 5 January Anne's illness was diagnosed as fatal. At the end of the month Charlotte sent the first volume of *Shirley* to Smith, Elder & Co. Sea air had been recommended for Anne, and on 24 May she set off for Scarborough accompanied by Charlotte and Ellen. On 28 May Anne died of tuberculosis at Scarborough and was buried at St Mary's Church on 30 May. Charlotte and Ellen moved to Filey and then to Bridlington. Charlotte was still writing *Shirley* and finished it on 28 August. It was published on 26 October.

1850 By now it was generally recognized that Currer Bell was in fact Charlotte Brontë, and from January the first tourists started to visit Haworth. From 6–9 March Charlotte stayed with Sir James and Lady Kay-Shuttleworth at Gawthorpe Hall, Padiham. In August she stayed with them again, this time at Briery Close, Bowness. Here she met her later biographer, Mrs Elizabeth Gaskell, for the first time. In December she stayed with Harriet Martineau, the famous critic, at her home, The Knoll, in Ambleside. During her visit Charlotte met the poet, Matthew Arnold.

1851 This was the year of the Great Exhibition. In June Charlotte visited the Crystal Place, then in Hyde Park, London. In November she started writing *Villette*.

1852 In early January Charlotte was very ill, unable to bend or to take solid food. During May and June she went to Filey to recuperate. She visited Anne's grave at Scarborough and found inaccuracies in the headstone engraving. On 20 November the final manuscript of *Villette* was sent to the publishers.

1853 In January Charlotte visited London again, staying with George Smith and his family. She corrected proofs of *Villette*. On 5 January she visited Newgate and Pentonville Prisons, the Bank of England and the Royal Exchange. *Villette* was published on 28 January, to be given a poor review by Harriet Martineau. By midsummer Charlotte had started writing *Willie Ellin*, a novel that would remain unfinished. In October she stayed with Miss Wooler at Hornsea, and by the end of November she was working on another novel, *Emma* (also to remain unfinished).

1854 On 3 April Charlotte became engaged to the Reverend Arthur Bell Nicholls, and she married him in Haworth Church on 29 June. The next day they went on honeymoon to Bangor, Wales, crossed to Dublin on 4 July and, after touring Ireland, returned to the Parsonage, Haworth, on 1 August.

1855 At the end of January Charlotte was found to be pregnant. On 17 February 'Tabby' the cook died.

Charlotte never regained her health and on 31 March she died of pthisis (consumption), and was buried in the vault below Haworth Church on 4 April.

1857 On 25 March Mrs Gaskell's biography of Charlotte was first published.

1861 The Reverend Patrick Brontë died on 7 June.

1879 With the exception of the tower, Haworth Church was demolished and rebuilt.

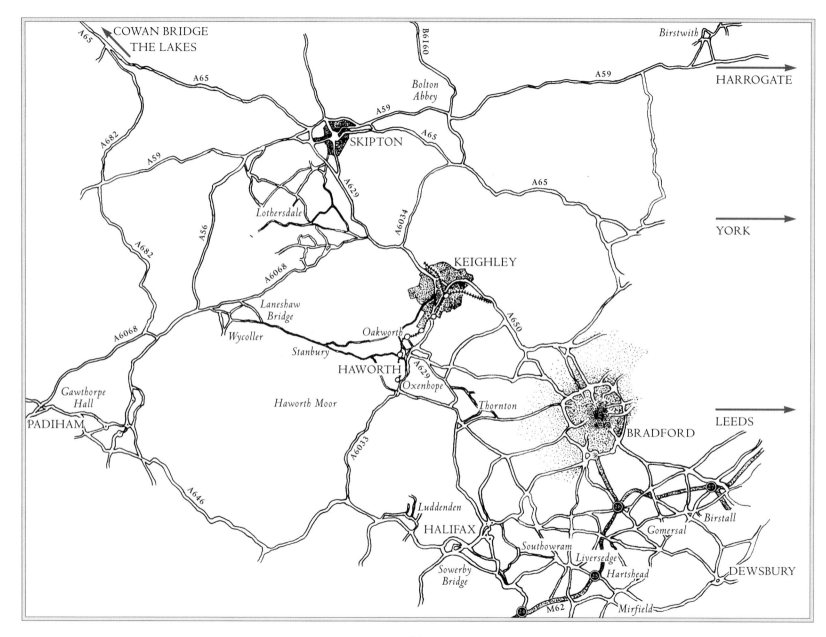

THE PLACES

LEFT: Haworth and surroundings.
RIGHT: The East Yorkshire Coast.

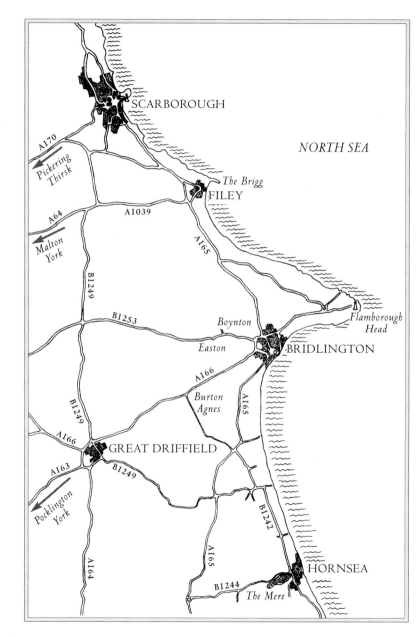

Hartshead and Hightown

The Reverend Patrick Brontë held the curacy at Hartshead prior to 1815. During his five years' incumbency he was appointed examiner at Woodhouse Grove School, where he met Maria Branwell, the niece of the headmaster, who was on a visit from Penzance.

❦

He married Maria in 1812, and their daughters Maria and Elizabeth were born at nearby Hightown, near Liversedge, in 1814 and 1815 respectively. These were troubled times in Yorkshire. Not only had the Napoleonic Wars resulted in a continental embargo, which hit the woollen industry and caused widespread unemployment at a time when new technology was being introduced to the mills, but the very changes gave rise to the revolutionary Luddites, who were determined to destroy the new machinery. Threat of rebellion caused Yorkshiremen to carry arms, and the Reverend Brontë continued to wear a brace of pistols at his belt until the day of his death, long after the disturbances had subsided. An Irishman by birth, his was not a docile nature. When the bell-ringers of Dewsbury Church had a practice session without his permission on a Sunday, he is reputed to have set about them with a cudgel.

Left: Hartshead Church.
Right: 25 Chapel Street, Penzance, home of Maria.

THORNTON

In May 1815, the year that Napoleon was finally defeated at Waterloo, the Reverend Brontë exchanged his living at Hartshead for that of Thornton in the parish of Bradford. The vicarage at Thornton, now a restaurant, was situated in Market Street, in the heart of the parish. It was to witness the births of the other Brontë children: Charlotte in April 1816, Branwell in June 1817, Emily in July 1818 and Anne in January 1820. Although much has since been built on to the building and the small garden where the children played has gone, much of the view that would have been familiar to the Brontës is unaltered today.

LEFT: Thornton Hall.
RIGHT: West Scholes Hall.

The parish then extended much further than it does now. Often accompanied by the children, their father would have travelled to Denholme, Clayton, Wilsden and Allerton, then separate villages, and to the many farms and hamlets around them, via footpath and track, over the moorland with its little valleys, tarns and farmsteads, green fields and enclosing dry-stone walls.

The vicarage had no water supply. The two maids, Sarah and Nancy Garrs, carried water from a communal trough in the town centre. One can picture the panic at times of childbirth. The front parlour served as delivery room, as was the custom, the large bed having been brought downstairs, and pans of water would have been set to boil on the kitchen range. The parlour can still be seen today.

Thornton supported a thriving industry in the angling line. Horse carcasses were allowed to putrefy in large troughs in the open, and the consequent infestations of blow-fly maggots provided a plentiful supply of bait for the tackle shops. The stench must have been something else.

Left: Vicarage, Thornton (74 Market Street)
Right: Upper Headley Hall.

HAWORTH

In April 1820 Patrick Brontë was appointed perpetual curate of Haworth. The living brought with it an improved stipend, a bigger, rent-free house for his family, and greater responsibilities. The day before Charlotte's fourth birthday, the Brontës travelled the rutted tracks over the moor from Thornton to Haworth, in one of a convoy of seven rustic tumbrils carrying all their possessions, to the Parsonage that housed them for the rest of their lives.

For the mother and two elder daughters this destiny was fated to be a short one. As Charlotte was to write later, 'The scenery of these hills is not grand – it is not romantic; it is scarcely striking. Long, low moors – with heath, start in little valleys, where a stream waters, here and there, a fringe of stunted copse. Mills and scattered cottages chase romance from these valleys.'

Most of the houses in Main Street date from the time of the Brontës, built in the eighteenth and early nineteenth centuries to house textile workers. Rows of narrow windows (most of the cottages are typically three-storeyed) allowed light to reach the handlooms. The setts on the steep Main Street remain – cobbles laid horizontally to give sure footing to the horses.

LEFT: Haworth. RIGHT: Stanbury looking towards South Dean.

THE PARSONAGE

The Parsonage, built just before the turn of the nineteenth century, from local millstone grit, stands simple and four-square, exposed to the winds, surrounded on two sides by the grave-yard, and with a commanding view of the Worth Valley and the moors. It is now a well-appointed museum and a must for Brontë enthusiasts. The rooms are arranged much as they were when the family lived here. The early days must have been dreadfully clouded by the terminal illness of Maria, no doubt exacerbated by the birth of five children in just over as many years and by the upheaval of the move from Thornton when Anne was but three months old. Maria died in September 1821, less than eighteen months after her arrival in Haworth.

The imagination can people the house as it was in happier times. The Brontës' aunt, Miss Branwell, wearing a lace cap and with her feet in wooden pattens as a safeguard against the damp and the stone floors, became housekeeper and a rather austere mother to the children, who were known nevertheless to tease her at times. Maria, the eldest, all of eight years old in 1821,

took on the role of mother to the younger children, and in the 'children's study' upstairs would shut herself in with a newspaper to read the parliamentary debates. As in most Yorkshire homes, the kitchen was the hub of the house, presided over by the bustling 'Tabby', the cook Tabitha Aykroyd. Here the girls would help with the domestic chores – Charlotte sharp-tongued and dutiful, Anne dreamily 'pilloputating' (peeling potatoes), and Emily baking the bread. There were dogs, geese, even a hawk called Hero, and Jasper the pheasant. Samplers were sewn, music practice obediently observed, along with drawing – especially by Branwell – and, always, writing: journals, diaries and the romantic histories of imaginary countries, landscapes and their inhabitants, prompted by the books and poetry they read.

❧✦❧

ABOVE: Haworth.
LEFT: The Parsonage at Haworth.

THE CHURCH AND CHURCHYARD

The church tower is all that remains of St Michael and All Angels, Haworth, where the Reverend Brontë preached. In 1879, eighteen years after his death, the rest of the church was demolished and rebuilt. The original church, according to Mrs Gaskell, Charlotte's contemporary biographer:

claims greater antiquity than any other in that part of the kingdom; but there is no appearance of this in the external aspect ... The interior of the church is commonplace; it is neither old enough nor modern enough to compel notice.

All the Brontës, with the exception of Anne, who lies at Scarborough, are buried in a vault beneath the present church. A wall monument to them was carved by the sexton, John Brown, a friend of Branwell, and is now in the memorial chapel. The huge, three-tiered pulpit from which Patrick Brontë preached has gone, but the top tier is still in use in the church in nearby Stanbury.

It is to Ellen Nussey, Charlotte's lifelong friend, that we owe a sombre picture of the churchyard. In spite of Patrick Brontë's strenuous efforts to improve the sanitary conditions prevailing in Haworth, the village:

refused to acknowledge the real remedy for prevalent sickness and epidemic. The passing bell was often a dreary accompaniment to

LEFT: Haworth Church.

the day's engagements, and must have been trying to the nervous temperaments of those who were always in sound of it as the Parsonage inmates were, but every thing around, and in immediate vicinity, was a reminder of Man's last bourn: as you issued from the Parsonage gate you looked upon the stone-cutter's chipping shed piled with slabs ready for use, and to the ear there was the incessant sound of the chip, chip of the recording chisel as it ground in the dates of births and deaths.

Even at this date the graveyard was crowded with tombstones, almost to the exclusion of any intervening turf. To the fury of the parson, the Haworth housewives had long considered it their abiding right to hang their washing out on the gravestones to dry. When he finally succeeded in expelling them, the Reverend Brontë tempered his triumph with humour:

The females all routed have fled with their clothes
To stockyard and backyards: where no one knows
And loudly have sworn by the suds that they swim in
They'll wring off his head for his *warring with women* ...

For a reputedly dour man, who loaded his pistol in the bedroom every night and unloaded it by discharging it every morning, such wit shows a facet of his character that is delicious by contrast.

Apothecary's Shop

This is the apothecary's shop where Branwell obtained his supply of laudanum (opium, then sold over the counter as a painkiller), which contributed so greatly to his untimely death. The dangers of opium addiction were not recognized in those days, and as an intoxicant it was far less expensive than spirits. Thomas De Quincey, in his popular book *The Confessions of an English Opium-eater*, recommended the drug as a preventative against consumption, fear of which disease could also have contributed to the start of Branwell's habit.

✦✧✦✧✦

LEFT: *The Apothecary's Shop, Haworth.*

THE BLACK BULL

When at home, Branwell spent much of his time at the Black Bull, carousing with his friends or taking boxing lessons. In his early youth he was a witty and stimulating companion, and many a time the landlord would send for him to entertain visitors staying at the inn. In later years it is said that Emily used to collect him of a night when his wits and legs became too fuddled to steer him safely home.

Outside the pub, his father was an impassioned orator in support of Robert Peel and the Tories in the hustings of 1835. Not content with rowdy heckling, the villagers burnt him in effigy, with a herring in one hand and a potato in the other.

RIGHT: The Black Bull, Haworth.

THE SUNDAY SCHOOL

The Reverend Brontë was instrumental in the building of the first Sunday School in Haworth in 1832. He also raised the money for the first organ and the first bell in the church. Charlotte taught at the school, as did Branwell for a time, though he proved to be an irascible and intolerant teacher.

❧⟡❧

... In the red fire's cheerful glow.
I think of deep glens blocked with snow;
I dream of moor and misty hill,
Where evening closes, dark and chill.
EMILY, *FAITH AND DESPONDENCY*, 1846

❧⟡❧

LEFT: The Sunday School, Haworth.
RIGHT: Oldfield.

THE MOORLAND

In all the lonely landscape round
I see no sight and hear no sound,
Except the wind that far away
Comes sighing o'er the heathy sea.

EMILY, THE SUN HAS SET, 1846

More fitting than the tomb where they are buried, or the house where they lived, the moorland surrounding Haworth is the true shrine of the Brontë sisters. From a very early age they were out in most weathers, and they knew every rock and stream, every mound and hollow. The days were sad when conditions were just too hostile to venture out on their beloved moors. Witness the famous opening lines of *Jane Eyre*:

There was no possibility of taking a walk that day ... the cold winter wind had brought with it clouds so sombre, and a rain so penetrating, that further outdoor exercise was now out of the question.

Wuthering: 'a significant provincial adjective, descriptive of the atmospheric tumult ... in stormy weather.'

EMILY, WUTHERING HEIGHTS

RIGHT: Barn on Haworth Moor.

I know groups of trees that ravish the eye with their perfect, picture-like effects.

CHARLOTTE, SHIRLEY

LEFT: Barn on Haworth Moor.

✣✦✣

... the twilight of close-ranked trees.

CHARLOTTE, *JANE EYRE*

✣✦✣

RIGHT: Woods at Dean Fields.

A little and a lone green lane
That opened on a common wide;
A distant, dreamy, dim blue chain
Of mountains circling every side

EMILY, A LITTLE WHILE, 1838

And behold, with tenfold increase blessing
Spring adorned the beauty-burdened spray;
Wind and rain and fervent heat caressing
Lavished glory on that second May.

EMILY, DEATH, 1845

The still May morn is warm and bright,
Young flowers look fresh and grass is green,
And in the haze of glorious light
Our long, low hills are scarcely seen.

EMILY, A.G.A. TO A.S., 1838

LEFT: Lane with foxgloves.
RIGHT: Buttercup field, West Scholes.

If thou be in a lonely place,
If one hour's calm be thine,
As evening bends her placid face
O'er this sweet day's decline;
If all the earth and all the heaven
Now look serene to thee,
As o'er them shuts the summer even,
One moment – think of me!

CHARLOTTE, *Stanzas*, 1845

❧❦❧

… the pleasantest manner of spending a hot July day was lying from morn till evening on a bank of heath in the middle of the moors, with the bees humming dreamily about the bloom, and the larks singing high up overhead, and the blue sky and bright sun shining steadily and cloudlessly.

EMILY, *Wuthering Heights*

❧❦❧

Left: Bully trees
Right: Dean Fields.
Overleaf: Top Withens.

… the moors seen at a distance, broken into cool, dusky dells;
close by great swells of long grass undulating in waves to the breeze.

EMILY, *Wuthering Heights*

... woods and sounding water and the whole world awake and wild with joy.

EMILY, *WUTHERING HEIGHTS*

✤✣✤✣✤

I've seen the purple heather-bell
Look out by many a storm-worn stone;
And oh, I've seen such music swell,
Such wild notes wake these passes lone.

EMILY, *A FAREWELL TO ALEXANDRIA*

✤✣✤✣✤

Oh! I might sing of pastures, meads and trees
Whose verdent hue is tinged with solar beams;

CHARLOTTE, *MATIN,* 1830

✤✣✤✣✤

LEFT: Colne Water, Parson Lee.
RIGHT: Dove Stones Moor.

A heaven so clear, an earth so calm,
So sweet, so soft, so hushed an air
And, deepening still the dream-like charm,
Wild moor sheep feeding everywhere.

EMILY, *A LITTLE WHILE,* 1838

❧✦❧

Morn comes and with it all the stir of morn,
New light, new life upon its sunbeams borne.

BRANWELL, *MORNING,* 1834

❧✦❧

The damp stands in the long, green grass
As thick as morning's tears.

EMILY, *MILD THE MIST,* 1839

❧✦❧

LEFT: Dike Nook.
RIGHT: Barn on Ponden Clough.

At length the air 'gan brighten; faint there shone
A rainbow path through all the expanse of blue.

CHARLOTTE, *THE VISION* (A SHORT POEM), 1830

✦✦✦✦✦

Where the grey flocks in ferny glen are feeding
Where the wild wind blows on the mountain side.

EMILY, *OFTEN REBUKED*, FIRST PUBLISHED 1850

✦✦✦✦✦

Sit still – a breath, a word may shake
The calm that like a tranquil lake
Falls settling slowly o'er my woes;
Perfect, unhoped-for sweet repose …

CHARLOTTE, POEM, C. 1837

✦✦✦✦✦

LEFT: *Sheep on Haworth Moor.*
RIGHT: *Stream and rainbow on Haworth Moor.*

Where the sun had gone down in simple state ...
spread a solemn purple, burning with the light of
red jewels and furnace flame at one point, on one
hill-peak, and extending high and wide, soft and
still softer, over half heaven.

CHARLOTTE, *JANE EYRE*

✵✵✵✵✵

For the moors, for the moors where the short grass
Like velvet beneath us should lie!
For the moors, for the moors where each high pass
Rose sunny against the clear sky!

EMILY, POEM, 1838

✵✵✵✵✵

The mute bird sitting on the stone,
The dank moss dripping from the wall,
The garden walk with weeds o'ergrown,
I love them – how I love them all!

EMILY, *A LITTLE WHILE,* 1838

✵✵✵✵✵

*LEFT: View from Penistone Hill of Stanbury and
Oakworth Moor.*
RIGHT: Pond and bog on Haworth Moor.

The rugged bank and rippling brook were treasures of delight. Emily, Anne and Branwell used to ford the streams, and sometimes placed stepping stones for the other two; there was always a lingering delight in these spots – every moss, every flower, every tint and form, were noted and enjoyed. Emily especially had a gleesome delight in these nooks of beauty – her reserve for the time vanished. One long ramble made in these early days was far away over the moors to a spot familiar to Emily and Anne, which they called 'the Meeting of the Waters'. It was a small oasis of emerald green turf, broken here and there by small clear springs; a few large stones served as resting places; seated here we were hidden from the world, nothing appearing in view but miles and miles of heather, a glorious blue sky, and brightening sun. A fresh breeze wafted on us its exhilarating influence; we laughed and made mirth of each other, and settled we would call ourselves the Quartette. Emily, half reclining on a slab of stone, played like a young child with the tadpoles in the water, making them swim about, and then fell to moralizing on the strong and the weak, the brave and the cowardly, as she chased them with her hand.

ELLEN NUSSEY, CORRESPONDENCE TO MRS GASKELL

Awaken on all my dear moorlands
The wind in its glory and pride!
O call me from valleys and highlands
To walk by the hill river's side!

EMILY, POEM, 1838

⚜

Give we the hills our equal prayer,
Earth's breezy hills and heaven's blue sea;
We ask for nothing further here
But our own hearts and liberty.

EMILY, POEM, 1841

⚜

RIGHT: Brontë Falls.

Oh why, in the snow and storms of December
When branches lie scattered and strewn,
Do we oftest and clearest and brightest remember
The sunshine and summer of June?

BRANWELL, *MISERY, PART II,* 1836

✕✚✚✚✕

LEFT: Dean Fields.
ABOVE: Tree at Foster's Leap, near Wycoller.

The wild moorside, the winter morn,
The gnarled and ancient tree.

EMILY, *SONG BY JULIUS BRENZAIDA TO G.S.*

✕✚✚✚✕

Ever anon that wolfish breeze
    The dead leaves and sere from their boughs was shaking,
And I gazed on the hills through the leafless trees
    And felt as if my heart was breaking.

CHARLOTTE, *POEM,* 1835

... the whole hill-back was one billowy, white ocean; the swells and falls not indicating corresponding rises and depressions in the ground.

EMILY, *WUTHERING HEIGHTS*

⁂

But if the sunny summer time
And woods and meadows in their prime
   Are sweet to them that roam –
Far sweeter is the winter bare
With long, dark nights and landscape drear
   To them that are at home!

ANNE, 'LINES WRITTEN AT THORP GREEN', 1841

⁂

England might really have taken a slide up into the Arctic zone – The sky looks like ice, the earth is frozen, the wind is keen as a two-edged blade – I cannot keep myself warm.

CHARLOTTE, *LETTER TO ELLEN*

⁂

LEFT: Sun Hill.
RIGHT: Roms Greave.

Wild the road, and rough and dreary;
Barren all the moorland round;
Rude the couch that rests us weary;
Mossy stone and heathy ground –

EMILY, *SONG BY JULIUS BRENZAIDA*, 1838

✦✦✦✦✦

But lovelier than cornfields all waving
In emerald and scarlet and gold
Are the slopes where the north-wind is raving
And the glens where I wandered of old.

EMILY, *POEM*, 1838

✦✦✦✦✦

Shadows on shadows advancing and flying,
Lightning bright flashes the deep gloom defying,
Coming as swiftly and fading as soon.

EMILY, *POEM*, 1836

✦✦✦✦✦

LEFT: Dove Stones Moor.
OVERLEAF: Haworth Moor at dusk.

TOP WITHENS

Top Withens, or Higher Withens, is a ruined farmhouse high on Haworth Moor. Although the name is associated with *Wuthering Heights,* the building, even in its pristine state, could never have been the model for the house where the Earnshaws lived. The setting, however, is just right, and it is generally agreed that Emily used it as the site for Wuthering Heights, even though that house is a composite built from memories of more august dwellings.

❧❧❧❧

LEFT: Top Withens.

STANBURY

Isolated by both the remoteness of their village and the very real barriers of class and intellectual refinement that pertained in those days, the Brontë children had very few acquaintances nearby whom they could visit socially. Branwell had a freer reign and was innately ebullient and outgoing, but the girls were very much dependent on their own company. Naturally shy, their nervousness of strangers and, in Emily's case, often apparently rude withdrawal are understandable.

LEFT: The Old School, Stanbury.
RIGHT: Stanbury.

The Taylor family, however, lived in the manor house at nearby Stanbury, about two miles west of Haworth. These were not the Taylors of Charlotte's schoolfriend, Mary, but the family of one of Reverend Brontë's church trustees. They were quite close to the Brontës, and the Reverend Brontë often used to preach at Stanbury Church.

Other orators whom the church had welcomed were the renowned William Grimshaw, his predecessor at Haworth, and Charles and John Wesley. When Haworth Church was pulled down in 1880 prior to rebuilding, the great three-tiered pulpit was dismantled, and the top tier can still be seen in Stanbury Church.

On Stanbury Moor, in September 1824, just after Charlotte had departed for Cowan Bridge School, the three younger children were exploring when a cataclysmic landslip nearly cost them their lives. A bog erupted and slid down the hillside, carrying trees, rocks and much earth and water with it. This was a fertile source of sermonizing for Reverend Brontë, who used the natural disaster as the basis for a poem for the Sunday School, a salutary diatribe from the pulpit and a lesson for his children in the omnipotence of the Creator.

LEFT: Stanbury.
RIGHT: Stanbury Church.

PONDEN HALL

About a mile and a half beyond Stanbury, past the Old Silent Inn, lies Ponden Hall. This was the home of the ancient Heaton family, of whom two members were hereditary trustees of Haworth Church. The Brontës used to make regular visits here, and it is certain that the children had access to the extensive library. Its amazing collection included a Shakespeare First Folio and much sixteenth- and seventeenth-century English and French literature. Branwell's early drama, *The Poetaster,* is self-consciously Jacobean in style, and Charlotte's verse at the age of fourteen or thereabouts has similar echoes.

The original house was built in 1513, and it was extensively rebuilt in 1801. The date may have been significant for Emily – it is the first word in *Wuthering Heights.* The house is indeed often taken for Thrushcross Grange. Once again, the site is right, but the building lacks the graciousness and parkland setting that Emily describes. It could more easily be likened to *Wuthering Heights* itself.

⚜

LEFT: Ponden Hall.

PONDEN KIRK

A conspicuous outcrop of rock to the west of Stanbury Moor is known as Ponden Kirk. A beck, with a series of little falls, descends from it down the ravine called Ponden Clough, and it can be reached from Ponden Hall. The whole panorama, beloved of Emily, is redolent of *Wuthering Heights*. The rocks became Penistone Crags, the narrow passage beneath them, the Fairy Cave, which so beckoned the young Cathy that one morning she 'leapt her Galloway over the hedge ... and galloped out of sight'.

ABOVE: *Ponden Kirk.*
RIGHT: *Ponden Clough.*

68

THE RAILWAY

Oxenhope was a village well known to the Brontës, but the railway up the Worth Valley from Keighley did not reach Oxenhope and Haworth in the Brontës' lifetime. It is idle to speculate on the difference it might have made to them, opening up easier opportunities to travel and widen their narrow world, and giving Branwell employment nearer the care of his family. Even then, however, the new railways were very much a part of the Brontës' lives. Emily was responsible for the investment of a small legacy left to them on the death of Aunt Branwell and she chose to speculate in railway shares on the advice of Miss Wooler – a naive choice of business manager, one is tempted to think, but Emily avidly read any paragraph and advertisement in the newspapers relative to the railroads, now steaming rapidly all over England, and her venture met with remarkable success.

In August 1840 Branwell got a job as a booking clerk. As Charlotte wrote to Ellen:

Patrick Boanerges has set off to seek his fortune in the wild wandering, adventurous, romantic, knight-errant-like capacity of clerk on the Leeds and Manchester Railroad.

Left: Steam train with Haworth in the background.
Above: Damens Railway Station.

Boanerges – the 'sons of thunder' – was originally the nickname ascribed to the Apostles, James and John, the sons of Zebedee. Despite her sarcasm, the railways were a powerful symbol of Victorian progress and the romantic Charlotte may secretly have seen her brother in a heroic mould. The adventurer became assistant clerk-in-charge at Sowerby Bridge, a post which, judging by the drawings and caricatures that ornamented his accounts, Branwell found prosaic enough.

In April 1841 he was promoted to clerk-in-charge at Luddenden Foot railway station, at a salary of one hundred and thirty pounds per annum. He stayed at the Lord Nelson, the inn in the village, where he made use of the 'library', the contents of which are still to be viewed at the pub.

❧❀❧

Left: Booking Hall, Oakworth Railway Station.
Above: Lord Nelson, Luddenden.

Alas, it was a questionable domicile for Branwell. He spent too many hours – even days – away from the office, regaling his friends in the bar. Finally, the company discovered a discrepancy of more than eleven pounds in the decorated account book.

Branwell was not accused of the theft – according to his friend Grundy, it was the porter, left alone in the office for so long, who purloined the cash – but in spite of a petition from his cronies in the village (where he was, not surprisingly, popular), as the responsible man in charge, he was dismissed.

LEFT: Haworth Station: the Worth Valley Railway is today a practical, working museum.

KEIGHLEY

Although Keighley was the nearest town within easy reach and must have figured largely in the lives of the Brontë family, there is little mention of it in surviving writings. A fragment of childhood diary written by Charlotte refers to the town in passing, but she is much more interested in the object of the errand:

> Keighley is a small town four miles from here. Papa and Branwell are gone for the newspaper, *The Leeds Intelligencer,* a most excellent Tory newspaper …

Keighley grew up from an original village with the coming of the Leeds–Liverpool Canal, and then in the mid-nineteenth century with the building of the railway. During the lifetime of the Brontës more than thirty mills were built, most of them on the banks of the River Aire and its tributaries.

Mrs Gaskell devotes the first chapter of her biography of Charlotte to the town, and she gives a vivid picture of a textile community mushrooming in the Industrial Revolution:

> Keighley is in the process of transformation from a populous, old-fashioned village, into a still more populous and flourishing town. As the gable-ended houses … fall vacant, they are pulled down to allow of greater space for traffic, and a more modern style of architecture.

Plus ça change! Today, just about the only surviving part of Keighley that the Brontës would still recognize is the site of the gates to the parish church and the adjoining pub, the Lord Rodney, at the end of North Street.

Keighley would have been the Brontës' nearest source of shops and a local market. It was also a source of reading material. Reverend Brontë did not join the Mechanics' Institute until after the girls had left their schooling at Roe Head, and only members could borrow books from the library, so it is doubtful whether that was an important source of their early reading material, as is often stated. There were, however, at least two Victorian circulating libraries, so popular with middle-class young ladies of the period, and there is reference from a contemporary to the girls walking in and out of Keighley to exchange their library books. Similarly, there is a contemporary account of Branwell's extravagant hilarity in a swing-boat at the fair during Keighley Feast, an annual tradition that continues today as Keighley Gala.

The walk in and out of Keighley would have been some ten miles altogether, downhill and uphill, following what is now the Worth Way. An arduous trek by modern standards, it was an expedition undertaken routinely, at least once a week, by the girls, in their long, incommodious Victorian skirts and petticoats. Most of the route has now become built up, but there are a few stretches that still show what the Worth Valley would have looked like when the Brontës were traversing it. The path that passes through the hamlet of Hainsworth is one instance.

The Cross Roads Inn near Barcroft was a pub frequented by Branwell, where he is reputed to have read *Wuthering Heights* to friends from Halifax.

❧

RIGHT: Lumb Foot, Worth Valley.

WYCOLLER

For many years a deserted village, Wycoller hides just over the Lancashire border, off the moorland road between Haworth and Laneshaw Bridge. The ruined Wycoller Hall is held to be the inspiration for Ferndean Manor in *Jane Eyre,* where Edward Rochester retreats after fire destroys Thornfield.

'Quite a desolate spot', it took Jane something of a trek to reach it:

I found myself at once in the twilight of close ranked trees. There was a grass-grown track descending the forest aisle between hoar and knotty shafts and under branched arches. I followed it, expecting soon to reach the dwelling, but it stretched on and on, it wound far and farther: no sign of habitation or grounds was visible.

LEFT AND ABOVE: Wycoller.

*F*erndean was:

A building of considerable antiquity … deep buried in a wood … uninhabited and unfurnished with the exception of some two or three rooms fitted up for the accommodation of the squire when he went there in the season to shoot.

✣

A dream that Jane describes earlier could well have been prompted by Wycoller – a dream that Thornfield Hall had become:

a dreary ruin, the retreat of bats and owls. I thought that of all the stately front nothing remained but a shell-like wall, very high and very fragile-looking. I wandered, on a moonlight night, through the grass-grown enclosures within: here I stumbled over a marble hearth, and there over a fragment of cornice.

✣

*E*mily, too, might have been thinking of Wycoller when she depicts the Old Hall of Elbe in an untitled poem:

House to which the voice of life shall never more return;
Chambers roofless, desolate, where weeds and ivy grow.

✣

ABOVE AND RIGHT: Wycoller

80

GAWTHORPE HALL

In March 1850 Charlotte went to stay with Sir James and Lady Kay-Shuttleworth at Gawthorpe Hall. The magnificent hall lies near Padiham in Lancashire, just off the present A671. The visit was a surrender to a sort of war of attrition waged by Sir James in an effort to get to know 'Currer Bell'. He was a remarkable man, a great social reformer; in his younger days, as a doctor in Manchester, he had battled against problems of hygiene among the poor and was instrumental in opening schools in workhouses. He lobbied tirelessly for free libraries and free education, and suffered a series of nervous breakdowns throughout his life due to overwork. He also had an artistic streak, which drew him to seek the company of writers. His interest had been aroused by the radical nature of Charlotte's novel *Shirley*.

LEFT: Gawthorpe Hall.

The publicity-shy Charlotte found Sir James uncomfortably overpowering, but the romantic in her was captivated by the monumental Jacobean hall with its reminiscences of her beloved Walter Scott, 'gray, antique, castellated and stately'. She failed to warm to his wife, whom she found graceless and without dignity. Whether or not she felt that Lady Kay-Shuttleworth's 200-year-old ancestry and her family's stately home (Sir James had taken her name, Shuttleworth, as the price of the inheritance) should have lent her aristocratic aloofness and condescension is not clear, but Charlotte found her hostess's kind attempts to be friendly 'painful and trying'. Their pressing invitation to stay with them in London over the season she described as a 'menace hanging over my head'. The truth was that, apart from her appalling nervousness in strange company, Charlotte had a deep dread of being patronized. Though never completely at ease, she was to thaw somewhat in her attitude to the Kay-Shuttleworths in later years.

✣

RIGHT: Gardens at Gawthorpe Hall.

ROE HEAD, MIRFIELD

In January 1831 Charlotte went to be formally taught at Roe Head, the girls' school run by Miss Margaret Wooler and her sisters at Mirfield Moor near Dewsbury. The event was a significant one for Charlotte. Not only was Miss Wooler to become a colleague and lifelong friend, but it was here that she met her two great friends, Ellen Nussey and Mary Taylor.

To Ellen (who later was to be the model for Caroline Helstone in *Shirley*) we owe most of our intimate acquaintance with the Brontë family at home, through her own accounts and diaries, and through the wealth of letters written to her by Charlotte throughout her life. Ellen kept this correspondence in defiance of Charlotte's instructions – on the orders of her husband, Mr Nicholls – to burn it.

The robust, cheerfully radical Mary Taylor gives us her first impression of meeting Charlotte, a new girl at the same time:

> She looked a little, old woman, so short-sighted that she always appeared to be seeking something … When a book was given her she dropped her head over it till her nose nearly touched it, and when she was told to hold her head up, up went the book after it, still close to her nose, so that it was not possible to keep from laughing.

RIGHT: *Roe Head School, Mirfield.*

Charlotte's sister-pupils were the daughters of the newly affluent mill families, and these gave her entrée to the big houses in the area, many of which appear, lightly disguised (if at all), in the novels. The chimneys of their paternalistic mills were visible beyond the trees at Roe Head, as she described in *The Professor:*

> Tall cylindrical chimneys, almost like slender, round towers … here and there mansions … occupied agreeable sites on the hillside; the country wore, on the whole, a cheerful, active, fertile look. Steam, trade, machinery had long banished from it all romance and seclusion. At a distance of five miles, a valley opening between the low hills held in its cups the great town of [Huddersfield]. A dull, permanent vapour brooded over this locality.

※※※

Charlotte returned to Roe Head as a teacher in 1835, bringing Emily with her as a pupil. Emily, however, was unable to tolerate a life of restriction away from the Parsonage and the freedom of the moors. She went home after three months, in imminent danger of a breakdown. Her place was taken by Anne, whose temperament was certainly more resilient and who remained a pupil at the school for the next two years.

※※※

Left: 'Mills of Huddersfield' (Armitage Bridge).

THE RED HOUSE

The Red House was the home of the Taylors; Mary, her parents and her brothers and sisters, the 'racy, vigorous Taylors', as Charlotte dubbed them. It stands just behind the road from Gomersal to Bradford. The house was originally built in 1660, low and gabled in red brick, and, like many of the 'wool barons' houses, was fashionably 'Italianized' in late Georgian times (many 'good old Yorkshire families' have Italianate surnames, stemming from the builders and artisans imported in those days). The changes included the addition of a gallery to the grand staircase in the hall, elegant mouldings and niches. The house and family were lifted virtually intact into *Shirley*, where the house became Briarmains and Mary's father evolved into Mr Yorke, together with his wife and brood of six children. The daughter, Rose, is an accurate portrait of Mary herself, who used to tease Charlotte that she had got the relative positions of the bedrooms all wrong.

One aspect of the interior that Charlotte describes in detail in the novel is a window;

seen by daylight to be brilliantly stained glass, purple and amber the predominant hues, glittering round a gravely-tinted medallion in the centre of each, representing the suave head of William Shakespeare, and the serene one of John Milton.

This window may now be seen at the Parsonage, in the Brontë Museum, Haworth.

RIGHT: The Red House.

RYDINGS, BIRSTALL

About three miles away from the Red House was Rydings, Ellen Nussey's home, where she lived with her widowed mother when she and Charlotte first met. It was a dignified, gritstone building with a castellated roof, surrounded by its own parkland with thorn trees, chestnuts and a rookery, lying off the Birstall to Halifax road. It certainly formed a major part, if not the whole, of the composite origin of Thornfield in *Jane Eyre*, which differs only in detail:

> Its gray front stood out well from the background of a rookery, whose cawing tenants were now on the wing. They flew over the lawn and grounds to alight in a great meadow from which these were separated by a sunk fence, and where an array of mighty old thorn trees, strong, knotty and broad as oaks, at once explained the etymology of the mansion's designation.

There was also, in company with other great houses, an associated legend of a mad woman and, more particularly, a grand old chestnut tree on the lawn, described (according to Ellen) by Branwell on a visit as 'iron-girthed, split by storms, but still flourishing in great majesty'. This tree was later to symbolize Rochester's tragedy:

> Descending the laurel walk, I faced the wreck of the chestnut tree: it stood up, black and riven: the trunk, split down the centre, gaped ghastly.

OAKWELL HALL

Nearby in Birstall another significant house, owned by relations of the well-connected Nusseys, was the august Elizabethan Oakwell Hall. Charlotte must have visited with Ellen on more than one occasion, for it was to become the residence of Shirley Keeldar, 'the old and tenantless dwelling yclept Fieldhead'. As Charlotte described it in *Shirley:*

> ... it might at least be termed picturesque. Its regular architecture, and the gray and mossy colouring communicated by time, gave it a just claim to this epithet. The old latticed windows, the stone porch, the walls, the roof, the chimney stacks, were rich in crayon touches and sepia lights and shades. The trees behind were fine, bold and spreading; the cedar on the lawn in front was grand; and the granite urns on the garden wall, the fretted arch of the gateway, were, for an artist, as the very desire of the eye.

Charlotte also re-creates the dark, twisted Jacobean furniture and the sinister dark oak, where 'fine, dark glossy panels compassed the walls gloomily and grandly', but her practical experience of housekeeping at home renders her not uncritical. She allows it to be very handsome:

> but – if you know what a 'spring clean' is – very execrable and inhuman. Whoever ... has seen servants scrubbing at those polished wooden walls with beeswaxed cloths on a warm May day must allow that they are 'intolerable and not to be endured', and I cannot but secretly applaud the benevolent barbarian who had painted ... the drawing-room to wit, formerly also an oak room, of a delicate pinky-white, thereby earning for himself the character of a Hun, but mightily enhancing the cheerfulness of that portion of his abode, and saving future housemaids a world of toil.

Left: Oakwell Hall, Birstall.

LAW HILL, SOUTHOWRAM

Law Hill at Southowram, off the A58 two miles south-east of Halifax, housed the Misses Patchetts' boarding school for girls. In September 1837, on one of her rare absences from home, Emily went there as a music teacher. Never happy away from Haworth, she was worked to the limit, which added to her distress at this expensive seminary. As Charlotte wrote to Ellen:

> Hard labour from six in the morning until near eleven at night, with only one hour of exercise in between. This is slavery. I fear she will never stand it.

The situation was not apparently without its dividends. The surrounding high moorlands were more or less the landscape of home. The house and courtyard were built in the latter half of the eighteenth century by one Jack Sharp, and it is likely that he provided to some extent a model for the surly Heathcliff. He had been adopted by an uncle, whose business he had acquired by sundry unscrupulous means, and his character and general demeanour were manifestly mirrored in Emily's infamous anti-hero, to be created some ten years after she had left Law Hill. Certainly, Emily would have known of Sharp, and of his reputation. And a servant, one Mrs Earnshaw, is known to have been employed at the school.

Near Law Hill, overlooking the beautiful Shibden Valley, stood a castellated Jacobean mansion, High Sunderland Hall, falling to ruin in Emily's time and now demolished. It had an elaborately decorated gateway in a high wall, with carved stone griffins and heraldic devices. As Mr Lockwood states on first seeing *Wuthering Heights*:

> I paused to admire a quantity of grotesque carving lavished over the front, and especially about the principal door, above which, among a wilderness of crumbling griffins and shameless little boys, I detected the date 1500 and the name Hareton Earnshaw.

QED?

RIGHT: Law Hill, Southowram.

BOLTON ABBEY

In the late summer of 1833 Ellen Nussey had been staying with the family at the Parsonage, her first of many visits to Haworth. In the course of her return to Birstall, it was planned for them all to travel with her on a day out to Bolton Abbey, where she would meet her own family and drive home with them. They all went shares of their meagre pocket-money and Branwell hired a rather shabby double gig with a driver. They set off for the famous beauty-spot between five and six in the morning, Branwell showing off his brilliant memory by naming all the hills along their route and their heights above sea-level.

When they arrived at the Devonshire Arms, the ostlers reportedly looked down their noses at the occupants of the dilapidated carriage, but revised their opinions when the smart Nussey equipage drew up and the two parties proved to be friends. After breakfast they all visited the ruins of the Priory and its surroundings. Emily and Anne were overcome with shyness, but Branwell was on particularly scintillating form, quoting poetry to an appreciative audience and charming all with his fascinating conversation.

There is no record of further visits to Bolton Abbey, but Charlotte was undoubtedly to re-create it in the 'Nunnely' of Sir Philip in *Shirley*:

… its old church, its forest, its monastic ruins. It also had its hall, called the priory … and what is more, it had its man of title.

Alluding further to the Cavendish family:

The present baronet, a young man hitherto resident in a distant province, was unknown on his Yorkshire estate.

Charlotte has Shirley Keeldar describe to Sir Philip the details of this impressive place:

the antique priory, the wild sylvan park, the hoary church and hamlet; nor did she fail to counsel him to come down and gather his tenantry about him in his ancestral halls. Somewhat to her surprise, Sir Philip followed her advice to the letter, and, actually, towards the close of September, arrived at the priory.

… he made parties for her to his own grounds, his glorious forest; to remoter scenes — woods severed by the Wharfe, vales watered by the Aire.

RIGHT: Bolton Abbey.

BIRSTWITH
SWARCLIFFE HALL

In the May of 1839 Charlotte went as nursery governess to the Sidgwick children at Stonegappe, Lothersdale. Governessing was not a job she liked; she lacked the patience to cope happily with small children, and she disliked the status accorded to a governess: disdain and condescension from employers, jealousy and resentment from the servants, neither upstairs nor downstairs, or, as she put it, 'neither flesh nor fowl, nor good red herring'. Family finances, however, demanded that she take a job, so to a job she went.

The house, still standing and well visible from the valley below, was re-created in *Jane Eyre* as Gateshead, where also may be found the children: 'More

LEFT: Swarcliffe Hall, Birstwith.
RIGHT: St James Church, Birstwith.

riotous, perverse, unmanageable cubs never grew.' Charlotte enjoyed the surrounding countryside, however, which was rather more wooded than at home.

Even more unlike the Haworth landscape were the surroundings of Swarcliffe Hall, Birstwith, a few miles from Harrogate. Here lived Mrs Sidgwick's father, John Greenwood, and the family moved there *en masse* for the summer. The house with its spire is immediately recognizable and commands picturesque views across the dale. The Vale of Nidd is a lush, fertile, agricultural valley and the change from dry-stone wall to fence and flower-filled hedgerow is a dramatic one. The visual aspect, as always, appealed to Charlotte, who described it as 'a beautiful place in a beautiful country'. The family and relations she wickedly caricatured years later in *Jane Eyre* as the Ingrams and friends – proud, loud and callous – who accompanied Rochester on one of his sudden returns to Thornfield.

Norton Conyers

*I*n extensive grounds outside the village of Wath, just north of Ripon, stands Norton Conyers, the Jacobean home of the Graham family since 1624. It is claimed that Charlotte visited the house with the Sidgwick family when, as the children's governess, she was staying at Swarcliffe Hall, Birstwith. It is not the only instance of a single visit so impressing itself on Charlotte's amazingly retentive memory that details are reproduced years later in her novels, and the house bears so many similarities to Thornfield Hall that the claim would seem to be partially justified. It seems likely that Thornfield is a composite of at least three houses (the other two probably being Rydings at Birstall and North Lees Hall, Hathersage), and this may well be one of them. And, in common with other old houses, there was a room in the attic where family tradition held that a mad woman was once incarcerated.

LEFT AND RIGHT: Norton Conyers, near Ripon.

COWAN BRIDGE

*I*n Cowan Bridge, on the side of the A65 just south of Kirkby Lonsdale, stands the remaining, dormitory end of the school to which the elder Brontë sisters – Maria, Elizabeth, Charlotte and Emily – were sent in 1824. The building is now part of a row of cottages. A plaque on the roadside wall commemorates the children's brief attendance. The school, with its gardens, rooms and stern routine, is transformed into Lowood in *Jane Eyre*.

The views of the distant fells, notably Ingleborough, the Gragareth massif and Whernside to the east, the Luneside hills to the west, and the forest and hills of Bowland in Lancashire more distantly to the south, would all have been familiar landmarks to the Brontë girls.

Left: River below Whernside.
Right: Ingleborough.

Charlotte describes the bitter wind in January and February, which, 'blowing over a range of snowy summits to the north, almost flayed the skin from our faces'. By April, however, the hardships had lessened and she takes pleasure in a:

> prospect of noble summits girdling a great hill-hollow, rich in verdure and shadow; in a bright beck, full of dark stones and sparkling edges.

This is contrasted with the same beck:

> laid out beneath the iron sky of winter, stiffened in frost, shrouded with snow … That beck itself was then a torrent, turbid and curbless; it tore asunder the wood, and sent a raving sound through the air, often thickened with wild rain or whirling sleet: and for the forest on its banks, that showed only ranks of skeletons.

❧⟡❧

LEFT AND RIGHT: Wood and stream at Dean Fields.

On Sundays, whatever the weather, the schoolgirls used to walk to the church at Tunstall through the hamlet of Overtown. This was to become Brocklebridge Church in *Jane Eyre*. Today the church is usually open. The two miles from Cowan Bridge were considered too far to return between morning and afternoon services, so the pupils took a frugal lunch with them, which they ate in a small room above the main door of the church, now accessible only by ladder.

They returned by 'an exposed and hilly road', probably via the village of Leck. In the year of the Brontës' residence, the school was swept by an epidemic of typhoid (then styled 'low fever') as Charlotte describes in a letter to Miss Wooler:

> and consumption and scrofula in every variety of form that bad air and water, and bad, insufficient diet, can generate, preyed on the ill-fated pupils.

At Leck Church some of the ill-fated pupils are buried.

Maria was soon gravely ill with consumption (her portrait survives in the character of the patient, enduring Helen Burns) and Elizabeth's health was failing. On St Valentine's Day 1825 Maria was returned home to Haworth, and she died on 6 May. At the end of the month Elizabeth also came home, followed, thankfully, by Charlotte and Emily a few days later. Elizabeth died on 15 June.

❧

Left Tunstall Church. Right: Cottage in Tunstall Village.

HATHERSAGE

In 1845 Ellen Nussey's brother, Henry, married. He had recently become vicar of Hathersage, near the High Peak district of Derbyshire, about ten miles west of Sheffield. Ellen persuaded Charlotte to join her in July to prepare the vicarage for the home-coming bride and groom. Although the girls' stay lasted a mere fortnight – a fortnight spent happily organizing furniture and provisions, and airing and cleaning the house – the visit provided Charlotte with a wealth of images later to be used vividly in the novels.

Charlotte travelled by horse-drawn omnibus into the Derbyshire countryside, thrilled with the beauty of the hills and pastureland through which she passed. With a painter's eye for the scenic impact of landscape, she delighted in its variety and in the nuances of light and shade in the passing vista.

I struck straight into the heath; I held on to a hollow I saw deeply furrowing the brown moorside; I waded knee-deep in its dark growth; I turned with its turnings, and finding a moss-blackened granite crag in a hidden angle, I sat down under it. High banks of moor were about me; the crag protected my head: the sky was over that.

CHARLOTTE, *JANE EYRE*

ABOVE: Moors near Hathersage
RIGHT: Stanage Edge.

At the crossroads where the old road from Sheffield to Manchester bisected the north-south road from Yorkshire into Derbyshire, the old Moscar Cross once stood.

It must have been a landmark noted by Charlotte and Ellen during their rambles on the Hallam Moors in periods of respite from their housekeeping. Moscar Cross was to be remodelled into Whitcross, where the distraught Jane Eyre was dropped off by the coach, the extent of her fare spent, in her flight from Thornfield and her betrayal by Rochester.

… a stone pillar set up where four roads meet; whitewashed, I suppose, to be more obvious at a distance and in darkness. There are great moors behind and on each hand of me; there are waves of mountains far beyond that deep valley at my feet.

The roads have gone, though the A57 now runs just south of the old Sheffield-Manchester route. Beyond a farm now called Moscar Cross, remnants of the old road can be seen. And the view that Charlotte describes in *Jane Eyre* survives.

I heard a bell – a church bell. I turned in the direction of the sound, and there, amongst the romantic hills, whose changes and aspect I had ceased to note an hour ago, I saw a hamlet and a spire. All the valley at my right hand was full of pasture fields, and cornfields, and wood; and a glittering stream ran zigzag through the varied shades of green.

This was to become the village of Morton. The similarity to Hathersage is unmistakable even today.

LEFT: Stanage Edge, Derbyshire.
RIGHT: St Michaels Church, Hathersage.

Above the village, the famished Jane begged bread and cheese from a lonely farmhouse and, after a night exposed to the cold and damp, another farm provided some cold porridge that was destined for the pigs.

❧❦❧

LEFT AND ABOVE: Overstones Farm, Hathersage.

Overstones Farm could well be the site of the grange ('some calls it Marsh End, and some calls it Moor House') where, attracted by a distant light, Jane found refuge with St John Rivers and his sisters:

the purple moors behind and around their dwelling – the hollow vale into which the pebbly bridle-path leading from their gate descended, and which wound between fern-banks first, and then amongst a few of the wildest little pasture-fields that ever bordered a wilderness of heath, or gave sustenance to a flock of gray moorland sheep …

No doubt the busy preparations at the vicarage in Hathersage, in caps and aprons, keys at waist, airing the musty rooms and protesting at the damp, were to find echoes in those of the kind Mrs Fairfax of *Jane Eyre*, keeping everything at Thornfield prepared for the chance return of Mr Rochester. Certainly the church was to have its own repercussions: brasses, memorials and tombs abound to the Eyre family (Hathersage squires since the fifteenth century), and Charlotte and Ellen would have visited members of the family still living there.

❧❧

Left: Eyre headstone, Hathersage Church.
Right: St Michaels Church and Vicarage, Hathersage.

North Lees Hall

North Lees was the seat of the Eyres, surely another candidate for Thornfield:

> … of proportions not vast, though considerable; a gentleman's manor-house, not a nobleman's seat: battlements round the top gave it a picturesque look.

A large cupboard in North Lees caught the ever-observant eye of Charlotte, and she re-creates it in detail at Thornfield:

> A great cabinet opposite – whose front, divided into twelve panels, bore, in grim design, the heads of the twelve apostles.

A padded room was alleged to have been furnished for the first Mrs Eyre, who became mad. Like Rochester's demented wife, Bertha Mason, she also died in a fire.

LEFT: North Lees Hall, Hathersage.

LITTLE OUSEBURN

In March 1841 Anne Brontë left home to take up the post of governess with the Robinson family at Thorp Green Hall, Little Ouseburn, near the city of York. Surprisingly, it was the frail Anne, with her nervous stammer, who — unlike her sisters — had the stamina for such a job. The first to leave home originally, for a similar post near Mirfield, she was to remain at Little Ouseburn for over four years. Thorp Green was the 'big house' of a large estate, with woods, manors and farms, its own dairy and brewhouse, and stabling for fourteen horses. Anne was evidently happy there, and presumably she was 'good with children', which Charlotte manifestly was not. Certainly the two girls continued to write to their ex-governess for some time after she left.

RIGHT: Temple at Church, Little Ouseburn.

*H*er employers took Anne with them on summer seaside holidays, visits that were to bear fruit in her first novel *Agnes Grey*. The family is meticulously brought to life in the same book, especially the two girls, the one self-consciously beautiful and the other a hoyden, who frequently swore like a trooper. The house, now called Horton Lodge, is acknowledged to be 'a very respectable one', with park gates, a long drive and a stately portico. It has a wide park stocked with deer, and fine old trees and fertile fields, quiet green lanes and smiling, flower-scattered hedges. 'But it was depressingly flat to one born and nurtured among the rugged hills of [Haworth].' The church, attended twice on Sundays, required a two-mile drive in the family carriage, which always made Anne sick.

*I*n 1843 Anne found a post for Branwell as tutor to the elder Robinson boy. He was dismissed two years later for 'proceedings bad beyond expression'. That the proceedings have never been succinctly expressed by an unbiased source has resulted in a mystery so far incompletely solved. That some kind of an affair, however one-sided, existed between Branwell and Mrs Robinson is beyond dispute.

She was an attractive woman, older than Branwell, and 'certainly required neither rouge nor padding to add to her charms'; devoted to 'giving or frequenting parties, and in dressing at the very top of fashion'. No wonder Branwell was dazzled.

Mrs Gaskell hints at some unsavoury stories connected with her. Whether *affaire passionnelle* or mild flirtation, Branwell was convinced that he was in love with her, and she with him. It contributed without doubt to his subsequent slide into dissipation and decline, and Anne was sure that her former employer was directly responsible for his early death. She had relinquished her own post shortly before Branwell's return, when the daughters were presumably too old for the schoolroom.

LEFT: Holy Trinity Church, Little Ouseburn.

The Brontës in Lakeland

At the end of 1839 Branwell had obtained a position as tutor to the Postlethwaite family of Broughton House, Broughton-in-Furness, near Ulverston. This was one of his more successful ventures; he kept up a front of sober industry for months until he renewed acquaintance with Hartley Coleridge, the gifted son of the famous author of 'Kubla Khan', whom he had known in his days as a hopeful portrait-painter in Bradford. Coleridge invited Branwell to his cottage in Ambleside on May Day. They were both passionate devotees of poetry, and both dedicated topers (the latter addiction had cost Coleridge his Fellowship at Oriel).

Branwell was knocked off-kilter by the meeting, his 'first conversation with a man of real intellect in my first visit to the classic Lakes of Westmoreland', and his duties were thrown to the winds as he applied himself to verse-translation of Horace's first two books of *Odes*.

The environs of Windermere, encompassing Ambleside and Troutbeck, were not then the holiday centre and tourist attraction they have now become, but a retreat for poets and intellectuals, principal among whom were Wordsworth, Southey, Coleridge, De Quincey and Ruskin. Charlotte first visited the Lakes in 1850, the year after Anne's death. By this time the identity of 'Currer Bell' was no longer a secret, and she stayed with the Kay-Shuttleworths at Briery Close, near Bowness. Once again, though warmly welcomed by her hosts after a tiresome train journey, she went with reluctance. The visit, however, was to prove a landmark in Charlotte's life, for it was here that she first met Mrs Elizabeth Gaskell, fellow-novelist and a writer with a growing reputation, who was destined to become a substitute for Emily and Anne as confidante and eventually to be Charlotte's posthumous biographer.

Briery Close, the grounds of which are open to the public on bank holidays and midsummer Sundays, has a commanding site above Low Wood, with panoramic views over Lake Windermere, Coniston Fell, the Langdale Pikes and the hills above Ullswater. As Charlotte wrote:

The place is exquisitely beautiful, though the weather is cloudy, misty and stormy; but the sun bursts out occasionally and shows the hills and the lake.

In a letter to a friend, Mrs Gaskell wrote of her first impressions of Charlotte:

A little lady in a black silk gown ... she is undeveloped; thin and more than half a head shorter than I, soft brown hair not so dark as mine; eyes (very good and expressive looking straight and open at

RIGHT: Lakeland landscape, near Troutbeck.

you) of the same colour, a reddish face; large mouth and many teeth gone; altogether plain, the forehead square, broad and rather overhanging. She has a very sweet voice, rather hesitates in choosing her expressions, but when chosen they seem without an effort, admirable and just befitting the occasion. There is nothing overstrained but perfectly simple.

Mrs Gaskell's description, even allowing for the fashionable standards of beauty of a century and a half ago, seems rather uncharitable. The famous portrait of Charlotte by George Richmond (commissioned by her publisher, George Smith) was considered a faithful likeness by Ellen Nussey, who made efforts to obtain a reproduction for Mrs Gaskell, to illustrate the biography. Reverend Brontë, too, proclaimed it a 'correct likeness', though privately he thought it made her look much older. Whatever one's taste, the piquante, intelligent little face can in no way be called plain.

✖✦✖

Charlotte was given a carriage tour of the countryside, which, used to roaming the moors at home, she found frustrating. A carriage (as opposed to an open-carriage) was enclosed, and it must have been like viewing the scenery through the windows of an Austin Seven. She described it in a letter to Miss Wooler:

I find it does not agree with me to prosecute the search of the picturesque in a carriage. A waggon, a spring-cart, even a post-chaise might do – but the carriage upsets everything. I longed to slip out unseen, and to run away by myself in amongst the hills and dales. Erratic and vagrant instincts tormented me, and these I was obliged to control, or rather suppress – for fear of growing in any degree enthusiastic, and thus drawing attenton to the 'lioness', the authoress – the she-artist.

✖✦✖

Friendship grew between Charlotte and Elizabeth Gaskell. The morning after the latter's arrival, they went out on the lake in a rowing boat from the landing stage that belonged to the house. They discovered they had a mutual admiration for the works of Newman and Ruskin. In the afternoon, to Mrs Gaskell's excitement, a trip was arranged to nearby Coniston to meet Tennyson and his wife, who were staying there. They set off in the carriage with Sir James, who knew the Poet Laureate, outside on the box. Halfway there the rain started, and the health-conscious Sir James decided to turn back. This much annoyed Mrs Gaskell, who adored Tennyson's work, but Charlotte took it with equanimity, preferring Wordsworth, who had died a few months earlier at Rydal Mount.

The next day they were invited to tea with Mrs Arnold, widow of the great Rugby headmaster, Dr Thomas Arnold, at Fox How near Ambleside. Dr Arnold had built the house as a holiday home for himself and his family. Its charms appealed to Charlotte:

✖✦✖

RIGHT: Troutbeck, Lake District.
OVERLEAF: Elterwater, near Grasmere.

It was twilight as I drove to the place, and almost dark ere I reached it, but still I could perceive that the situation was lovely. The house looked like a nest, half buried in flowers and creepers; and dark as it was, I could feel that the valley and the fields around were beautiful as imagination could dream.

⁂

*I*n December of the same year, Charlotte visited the Lakes again, to stay with the famous critic, Harriet Martineau, at her house, The Knoll, near Ambleside. She would have visited her friend during her earlier stay but, as she wrote:

Miss Martineau was away from home. She always leaves her home at Ambleside during the Lake Season, to avoid the influx of visitors to which she would be subject.

They had met originally in London, when Charlotte was staying with her publisher, George Smith, and his family. She had, prior to this, sent a copy of *Shirley* to Miss Martineau. Of *Jane Eyre*, the redoubtable Harriet said that she had guessed, from the description of Grace Poole sewing on curtain-rings, that the author, 'Currer Bell', was either a woman or an upholsterer. Her reviews of Charlotte's work were appreciative and favourable.

With a large ear-trumpet as a hearing-aid, Harriet was eccentric to a degree and visitors to The Knoll were encouraged to behave just as they pleased. She herself rose at five o'clock to a cold bath and a 'walk by starlight', and had finished breakfast and was at work at her desk by seven. Charlotte was for once completely at ease in the comfortable house with its unconventional routine, in spite of Sir James Kay-Shuttleworth's attempts to carry her off to Briery Close again. She parried these by driving with him in his carriage on most mornings.

Once again Charlotte visited the Arnolds at Fox How, and this time she met the doctor's son, Matthew Arnold, the poet, then in his early twenties. She had read Dr Arnold's *Life* in the interim and felt she knew the family well. Matthew Arnold wrote:

At seven came Miss Martineau and Miss Brontë (*Jane Eyre*); talked to Miss Martineau (who blasphemes frightfully) about the prospects of the Church of England, and, wretched man that I am, promised to go and see her cow-keeping miracles tomorrow — I who hardly know a cow from a sheep. I talked to Miss Brontë (past thirty and plain, with expressive grey eyes, though) of her curates, of French novels and her education in a school in Brussels, and sent the lions roaring to their dens at half past nine.

On the death of Charlotte, he was to enshrine Harriet and the whole Brontë family in a poem entitled 'Haworth Churchyard, April 1855'.

⁂

Right: Garden and view from Briery Close.

THE NORTH SEA COAST

In July 1839 Charlotte left the employ of the Sidgwick family at Stonegappe and returned to Haworth, thoroughly run-down and depressed. So much so that Ellen Nussey proposed a startling plan; they should both go, unchaperoned, for a seaside holiday. Their friend, Mary Taylor, suggested Burlington (now called Bridlington) on Yorkshire's North Sea coast. For two young ladies, both in their early twenties, such a daring venture was viewed with alarm. Objections were raised. Reverend Brontë considered it would demand too great an expense. Aunt Branwell expressed anxiety about the wind, the weather and the state of the roads. Added to which, the initial transport presented problems – the only gig for hire in Haworth was away in Harrogate for an indefinite period.

Charlotte proposed that she should walk the twelve miles to Ellen's home in Birstall. Her father would not hear of it. Boldly for her, Ellen cut the Gordian knot by simply arriving at the Parsonage in her brother's carriage and whisking her friend off to Leeds railway station. Brother Branwell applauded and proclaimed it 'a brave defeat ... the doubters were fairly taken aback'.

Charlotte had written earlier to Ellen:

Left: Cliffs near Filey

The idea of seeing the SEA – of being near it – watching its changes by sunrise, Sunset – moonlight – and noonday – in calm – perhaps in storm – fills and satisfies my mind.

They travelled from Leeds to Selby by train, which was as far as the railway had reached. For both of them it was their first exciting journey on this relatively new mode of transport. By coach, thence, to York, and from there in an 'open fly' to Driffield, where they stayed overnight at the Bell Hotel. Even now family concern was not to leave them be, for on arrival at Burlington they found, to their vexation, that Ellen's brother Henry had arranged for his friends, the Hudsons, to meet them and carry them off to their farmhouse at Easton, a couple of miles inland. The girls had counted on renting rooms by themselves at the seaside. They were mollified, however, by the kindness and generosity of their hosts. They were free to wander the countryside surrounding them, and Charlotte was later to refer to the stay as 'one of the green spots that I look back on with real pleasure'.

Bretton, the seaside town in *Villette*, is supposedly based on Old Burlington, much changed today. The friends spent much time exploring Boynton Woods (probably Harlequin Wood in the same novel), Burton Agnes and, of course, the seashore.

Easton House was demolished, not without protest, in 1961. Eastfield

131

Farm now occupies the site, alongside the 'York Scenic Route', near Boynton. There is a copy of a watercolour of the house, painted by Charlotte, in the Bayle Museum in Bridlington, and a Regency double seat originally from the house, with a book-box allegedly fitted for Charlotte's benefit.

✵✫✦✫✵

On the second day Charlotte insisted on a walk to the shore. Mrs Gaskell heard much later from Ellen about Charlotte's reaction on first seeing the sea: 'She could not speak till she had shed some tears – she signed to her friend to leave her and walk on.' Charlotte wrote to Henry Nussey:

> … its glories, changes, its ebbs and flow, the sound of its restless waves, formed a subject for contemplation that never wearied either the eye, the ear, or the mind.

Besides being in the mind's eye a constantly revisited source of literary inspiration, the East Yorkshire coast supplied a much-needed therapeutic balm for Charlotte at the times in her life when she was to benefit from it most.

✵✫✦✫✵

RIGHT: Filey Brigg.

SCARBOROUGH

During Anne Brontë's span as governess to the Robinsons in 1841 she spent the summer holidays with the family at Scarborough. This was her favourite resort.

She was later to describe the bustling seaside town vividly in her first novel *Agnes Grey*. Anne's style, though never as emotively poignant as Charlotte's, has a refreshing directness:

We were a considerable distance from the sea, and divided from it by a labyrinth of streets and houses. But the sea was my delight; and I would often gladly pierce the town to obtain the pleasure of a walk beside it . . . especially in the wild commotion of a rough sea-breeze, and in the brilliant freshness of a summer morning.

There was a feeling of freshness and vigour in the very streets, and when I got free of the town, when my foot was on the sands and my face towards the broad, bright bay, no language can describe the effect of the deep, clear azure of the sky and ocean, the bright morning sunshine on the semi-circular barrier of craggy cliffs surmounted by green swelling hills, and on the smooth wide, white sands, and the low rocks out at sea – looking, with their clothing of weeds and moss, like little grass-grown islands – and above all, on the brilliant, sparkling waves. And then, the unspeakable purity and freshness of the air!

The York-Scarborough railway was to open five years later, and it was not long before it brought a huge and constant influx of visitors from the large Yorkshire industrial towns. No longer a genteel watering-place and playground confined to the wealthier classes, Scarborough has a justifiable claim to be one of the first modern seaside resorts. The scene today is a different one from that of early morning in 1841, as depicted in *Agnes Grey*:

Still, there were only the early grooms with their horses, and one gentleman with a little dark speck of a dog running before him, and one water-cart coming out of the town to get water for the baths. In another minute or two, the distant bathing machines would start to move, and then the elderly gentlemen of regular habits, and sober Quaker ladies would be coming to take their salutary morning walks.

Anne was to revisit Scarborough under the most tragic circumstances. She had long suffered from a 'weak chest', and in January 1849 tuberculosis was diagnosed. It was suggested that she might benefit from the effects of sea air when the weather became milder. Anne was determined to see the sea again, and on 24 May, though she was too weak to walk downstairs and had to be carried, she set off for Scarborough with Charlotte and Ellen. They broke the journey at York, staying at The George, an old coaching inn in Whip-Ma-Whop-Ma Gate, the shortest street in the city. It is now the site of a building society office and a small paved area with seats. Anne, realizing more than the others that her end was near, was much calmed by the tranquil sight of York Minster.

The next day in Scarborough they stayed in a lodging house, No. 2, The Cliff, with a view of the bay. The Grand Hotel now stands there, and there is a commemorative plaque on the wall by the main entrance. Anne filled her time gazing at the sea from the large, airy room, and the following day they went driving on the sands in a donkey and cart. Anne died on 28 May, having exhorted her grief-sticken sister to 'Take courage, Charlotte; take courage.' By her own request, she was buried in St Mary's Churchyard on Castle Hill, where her memorial stone may still be seen.

❈❦❈❦❈

RIGHT: North Bay, Scarborough.

FILEY

Encouraged by Reverend Brontë, who was worried about the strain that Charlotte was under, she and Ellen stayed on at Scarborough for a while and then moved further down the coast to nearby Filey. As Charlotte wrote, 'It suits Ellen and myself better than Scarborough, which is too gay.' In those days Filey was a small fishing village, of little interest to the tourist, though an iron-impregnated 'chalybeate spring' was recommended to those who 'took the waters' for their health. This panacea was reputed to cure asthma, apoplexy and epilepsy, and it dried up a long time ago.

Charlotte and Ellen stayed at Cliff House in North Street, now Belle View Street, where the house is a shop and café. Interspersed by long walks and visits to Filey Brigg, the Coble landing and the beach, Charlotte worked on the third volume of the manuscript of *Shirley*. Chapter XXIV, 'The Valley of the Shadow of Death', is manifestly drawn from her grief at this time. As she wrote in a letter, 'Labour is the only radical cure for rooted sorrow.'

Above: A Coble; the traditional lug-sailed, flat bottomed fishing boat of the North Sea Coast.
Left: Cliffs near Filey.

Charlotte visited Filey again in the early summer of 1852. Illness and depression had taken their toll of her over the past year. Since the previous autumn she had been working on her new novel, *Villette*, and finding it heavy-going. The village was beginning to attract visitors, and by 1852 the first buildings had been built on The Crescent. Charlotte stayed again at Cliff House. The holiday was more in the nature of a melancholy pilgrimage, as she wanted to visit Anne's grave at Scarborough to ensure that the stonemason had done his work accurately. Sure enough, she found several mistakes on the stone, which had to be rectified, and this she put in hand. One yet remains; Anne was 29 when she died, not 28 as on the inscription.

⋇

Slowly the sea, the sunshine and the long walks in the fresh air, especially on the cliff path of Carr Naze and on Filey Brigg, combined to restore Charlotte's cheerfulness and bodily health. She even ventured to swim from 'a peculiar bathing contraption'. Again she wrote rapturously of the sea, though the weather was often far from placid: 'sea running mountains high … with great damage to the shipping and loss of life.'

⋇

LEFT: Bempton Cliffs.

FILEY BRIGG AND HORNSEA

Originally Filey Bridge, the name probably derives from a Scandinavian term meaning a landing place. According to legend, it was first built by the Devil in an attempt to bridge the North Sea. He stopped when his hammer fell out of his hand into the deep water. Trying to retrieve it, he mistakenly picked up a haddock, branding his fingerprints indelibly on the fish. The marks can still be seen on every haddock today and prove the truth of the tale.

The Brigg had a fascination for Charlotte, who spent many hours walking along its slippery length, as described in *Shirley*.

There tumbles in a strong tide, boiling at the base of dizzy cliffs. It rains and blows. A reef of rocks, black and rough, stretches far into the sea; all along, and among, and above these crags, dash and flash, sweep and leap, swells, wreaths, drifts of snowy spray. Some lone wanderer is out on these rocks, treading, with cautious step, the wet, wild sea weed; glancing down into hollows where the brine lies fathoms deep and emerald clear, and seeing there wilder and stranger and huger vegetation than is found on land, with treasure of shells – some green, some purple, some pearly – clustered in the curls of the snaky plants.

The last time Charlotte saw the East Yorkshire coast was in October of the following year. *Villette* had been published some seven months before, on the whole to favourable reviews, and the author was in better spirits for her final visit. An exception to the admirers was Harriet Martineau, who reacted coldly and carpingly to the book, for which Charlotte never forgave her. Miss Wooler had always been uneasy about Charlotte's friendship with the avowed atheist, and it was with Miss Wooler that she now stayed, in Hornsea, at 94 Newbegin, one of the earliest houses to be built to cater specifically for holiday-makers.

Hornsea, down the coast from Bridlington, is another little spa town, noted for its pottery. Nearby is Hornsea Mere, the largest freshwater lake in Yorkshire, where once two Yorkshire abbots, in a dispute over fishing rights, hired professional champions to fight the matter out. As usual, Charlotte spent most of her time there walking, by the lovely mere or on the sands of the shore.

RIGHT: Filey Brigg from Hunmanby Gap.

AFTERWORD

So our thoughts leave Charlotte on her beloved East Yorkshire coast gazing out at the North Sea, which never fails to fascinate and soothe her. Does she think of Brussels, way beyond the welkin's cheek, where the sky meets the watery horizon? Brussels, from where her innocent crush on M. Héger, her adored tutor, still tugs faintly at her heart-strings? Is the prospect balm enough for the grieving sister who has witnessed the cruel deaths of her siblings in pitiless and speedy succession; the demented Branwell; the passionate, obstinate Emily; the patient, submissive Anne?

Charlotte herself has little time to run – but another two years. To her discomfort she has already been 'lionized' in London, patronized by the demi-gods of the day; her 'great Turk and Heathen', the novelist W. M. Thackeray; John Millais, the Pre-Raphaelite painter and fashionable portrait artist. She has been fired by close glimpses of her childhood hero, the Duke of Wellington, and dazzled by the splendours of Joseph Paxton's Crystal Palace and the Great Exhibition of 1851, all of which she set down in letters home to her father.

The following year saw her engagement and marriage to the Reverend Arthur Bell Nicholls, and after a happy honeymoon in Ireland, Charlotte returned to Haworth, never to leave home again. Eight months later she was dead. Gone, leaving two unfinished novels and two lonely men, linked inseparably by her memory, to live out their remaining days in the empty gritstone Parsonage.

Left: Sunrise at Hunmanby gap.

143

No coward soul is mine,
No trembler in the world's storm-troubled sphere;
I see Heaven's glories shine
And Faith shines equal arming me from Fear.

EMILY BRONTË, 2 JANUARY 1846